Extravagant Generosity: The Heart of Giving

Program Guide

Extravagant GENEROSITY

The Heart of Giving

Program Guide

MICHAEL REEVES & JENNIFER TYLER

Foreword by Robert Schnase

ABINGDON PRESS
Nashville, Tennessee

EXTRAVAGANT GENEROSITY:
THE HEART OF GIVING

Program Guide

Library of Congress Cataloging-in-Publication Data

Reeves, Michael, Dr.
  Extravagant generosity : the heart of giving. Program guide / Michael Reeves and Jennifer Tyler.
       p. cm.
  ISBN 978-1-4267-2856-3 (printed book with cd/dvd insert : alk. paper) 1. Christian stewardship. I. Tyler, Jennifer. II. Title.
  BV772.R365 2011
  254'.8--dc22

                                                                                              2011008454

11 12 13 14 15 16 17 18 19 20--10 9 8 7 6 5 4 3 2
MANUFACTURED IN THE UNITED STATES OF AMERICA

CONTENTS

Foreword 7

About the Program 9

Introduction to the Program Guide 11

Biblical Foundation 13

Planning and Implementing the Program
    Step 1 Decide 17
        Present the Program to Leadership and Approve Dates

    Step 2 Assemble 19
        Form the Leadership Team

    Step 3 Prepare 24
        Equip the Leadership Team

    Step 4 Execute 25
        Complete the Planning Function

    Step 5 Implement 26
        Four Sundays of Worship, Preaching, Storytelling, and Teaching

            Sunday 1. EKG
            Ministry Flows from the Heart

            Sunday 2. The Art of Love
            Relationships Are Matters of the Heart

            Sunday 3. Bucket Lists
            Vision and Hope Are Inspirations of the Heart

            Sunday 4. Declarations of Your Heart
            Extravagant Generosity Is an Expression of Your Heart

Pastor and Program Director Checklist 31

Program Teams and Tasks

Communication Team 34
Leadership Summit Team 43
Worship and Teaching Team 51
Spiritual Emphasis Team 55

Resource CD-ROM Contents 60

FOREWORD

Giving helps us become what God wants us to be. God uses our generosity to reconfigure our interior lives, to create us anew, and to foster in us "the mind that was in Christ Jesus."

Congregations who seek to form people into followers of Christ have a responsibility to think deeply, prepare thoroughly, act wisely, and teach courageously about the relationship between faith and money. How does our giving affect our relationship to God? How does our relationship to God affect our giving? How does being a follower of Jesus shape all our behaviors concerning money—how it is earned, spent, saved, and offered to God?

Michael Reeves and Jennifer Tyler bring extraordinary insight, knowledge, and experience to the task of teaching and leading congregations as they address issues of faith and money. They have directed hundreds of local church annual and capital campaigns and have taught countless workshops and classes for congregations, conferences, and seminaries. The fruit of their ministry are lives changed by the practice of generosity and congregations flourishing in the ministry of Christ.

I'm grateful to God that Michael and Jennifer have created this excellent tool for congregations, *Extravagant Generosity: The Heart of Giving.* The step-by-step Program Guide and support materials include an array of resources to help pastors and lay leadership prepare, pray, lead, and follow through with a high-quality, theologically grounded, effective approach to practicing generosity. *Extravagant Generosity* changes the culture of the congregation from fundraising to generosity as a core value of discipleship.

I count it a privilege to work together with Michael and Jennifer, and I pray that this program blesses your congregation as we all seek to fulfill the mission God has given the church of making disciples of Jesus Christ for the transformation of the world.

Yours in Christ,
Robert Schnase

ABOUT THE PROGRAM

Extravagant Generosity: The Heart of Giving is a theologically sound, creative stewardship approach that is simple in design and built around functions that are easy to understand and implement. The objective of this program is, over time, to change the culture in your church from fund raising to generosity as a core value of discipleship. The effective methods and procedures can be used year after year to ultimately cultivate an environment of generosity. This program features tools for adults, youth, and children. Recognizing churches vary in technical ability, resources provided are adaptable, based on capability.

Program Steps

The program is planned and carried out in five steps, described in this Program Guide:

Step 1. Decide
Step 2. Assemble
Step 3. Prepare
Step 4. Execute
Step 5. Implement

These steps, begun by the pastor or church leadership, are carried out by a Program Director and Program Teams, and ultimately by all church members. When the planning is over and the groundwork has been laid, the program is implemented with the congregation over the course of four weeks, with four Sundays of special focus, including worship, sermons, and Sunday school or small-group activities. The fourth Sunday is Response Sunday, or Commitment Sunday.

In planning your schedule, allow four weeks for program implementation. A good way to do this is to pick a date for Response Sunday, then count back four weeks. That will determine the date of Sunday 1.

Program Components

Practicing Extravagant Generosity: Daily Readings on the Grace of Giving
A devotional guide written by Bishop Robert Schnase, designed to help everyone in your congregation understand and experience God's call to a life of Extravagant Generosity.

Program Guide with CD-ROM
An overview of the program's concepts, functions, and activities. The CD-ROM provides all the tools and materials you need to implement the program.

Timeline
A quick overview that reflects the steps, functions, and pulse of the program. It also serves as an orientation and ongoing guide for team leaders.

Small-Group and Worship DVD
Videos to help participants explore and encounter the grace of giving, to be used in worship and small-group settings.

Small-Group Leader Guide
A complete set of leader helps for the small-group sessions that take place in Sundays 1–4 of the program. Includes themes, Scriptures, DVD follow-ups, discussion questions, and prayers.

Planning Kit
Contains all of the items listed above, conveniently packaged together.

INTRODUCTION
TO THE PROGRAM GUIDE

One of the most difficult challenges for the church is effectively bringing the good news of Jesus Christ to a negative world in desperate need of something positive and transformational. The need for positive leadership seems more acute now than ever. The impact of the 24-hour news cycle in our culture seems to provide negative news on a wide variety of subjects. Political news is beleaguered by conflict and dysfunction rather than effective resolution of problems. Economic news is most often bleak and hopeless with rising bankruptcy numbers and increasing home foreclosures. Entertainment news regularly addresses the sensational moral failures of celebrities, and sports are often a composite of good stories offset by similar reports of personal demise and lack of sportsmanship. The negative world often has more influence on the church than the church has on presenting the good news to the world. This program is designed to celebrate what is right with the church by asking members to respond to the questions What do you love about your church?, Who in your church family has made a difference in your spiritual life?, and What is your vision and hope for your church?, and by encouraging a prayerful, positive response with an act of generosity.

As our culture continues to be affected by the aging of generations, changing economic realities, increased competition for charitable support, and a continually evolving vision for the church, a new approach to address personal generosity would be helpful. There is an apparent need to change from the traditional culture of fund raising in church to positioning generosity as a core value of discipleship and individual spiritual experience. There will never be enough fund-raising gimmicks to sustain significant giving in the church. Hearts must be encouraged so giving becomes an outpouring of one's love for God.

One resource that has helped define this change is *Consecration Sunday,* by Herb Miller. This program has been widely used and has often been very effective in helping church leaders motivate church members to give as part of their spiritual response to their personal need to give and not in response to underwriting a financial goal. *Extravagant Generosity: The Heart of Giving* is a fresh approach that identifies the positive attributes of a community of faith and builds upon them to communicate the message of generosity. Individual study, corporate worship, preaching, teaching, and storytelling conclude with an opportunity for people to express their love for God through their own generosity. This new approach is designed to encourage and provoke generosity.

The use of the word *generosity* is a part of the change in communication. Frequently, the word *stewardship* has been applied to the approach to finances in the local church. Unfortunately, that word carries negative "baggage." The word *generosity*, however, communicates the appropriate biblical and spiritual value. In his book *Five Practices of Fruitful Congregations,* Robert Schnase identifies Extravagant Generosity as one of the five fruitful practices. "The practice of generosity describes the Christian's unselfish willingness to give in order to make a positive difference for the purposes of Christ" (Abingdon Press, 2007, p. 112). He also says, "Generosity is a fruit of the Spirit, a worthy spiritual aspiration" (p. 116). This program guide is designed to walk church leaders through a step-by-step process to planning and implementing the program *Extravagant Generosity: The Heart of Giving.*

BIBLICAL FOUNDATION

A thread of recurring words from the Shema (Deuteronomy 6:4-5) forms the biblical basis for this program. In Mark 12:33 ("To love God with a whole heart, a full understanding, and all of one's strength, and to love one's neighbor as oneself is much more important than all kinds of burnt offerings and sacrifices"), and again in John 13:34 ("I give you a new commandment: Love each other. Just as I have loved you, so you also must love each other"), the great Shema is expressed in the context of the teachings of Jesus. The central issue is the wholehearted love of our God. In Paul's letter to church leaders in Corinth, he says giving is proof of our love for our Lord (see 2 Corinthians 8:24). In the famous verse of our faith about the very nature of God (John 3:16), we again see giving explained as an expression of love: "God so loved the world that he gave . . . ." The thread is also seen in other passages. We read in 1 Chronicles 29:9 that the people responded to the financial appeal from David "wholeheartedly" (NIV). Then in Matthew 6:21, Jesus says, "Where your treasure is, there your heart will be also." And looking again to Paul's letters to the church at Corinth, Paul suggests that generosity, as reflected by the Macedonians, came from first giving themselves to the Lord (See 2 Corinthians 8). They made a spiritual decision. In addition, Paul says, "Everyone should give whatever they have decided in their heart" (2 Corinthians 9:7).

Without more insightful teaching about what constitutes meaningful life, the prevalent cultural momentum of acquisition, consumption, and accumulation of possessions becomes our default value. First Timothy 6:17-19 provides an important framing passage:

> *Tell people who are rich at this time not to become egotistical and not to place their hope on their finances, which are uncertain. Instead, they need to hope in God, who richly provides everything for our enjoyment. Tell them to do good, to be rich in the good things they do, to be generous, and to share with others. When they do these things, they will save a treasure for themselves that is a good foundation for the future. That way they can take hold of what is truly life.*

Generosity, not consumption, is a key value of a meaningful life.

Tithing

There is one other matter that should be explored in preparation for the *Extravagant Generosity: The Heart of Giving* program. Tithing is a relevant theological issue that must be considered. Tithing is first mentioned in Genesis 14:20, " 'and blessed be God Most High, who has delivered your enemies into your hand!' And Abram gave him one tenth of everything" (NRSV). But the idea of tithing is not unique to the Old Testament or Mosaic Law. Tithing is found as a key principle in the history of many cultures. This tithe was a one-tenth portion of income or available resources. In the Old Testament, there were three kinds of tithes. In Leviticus 27:30-32, a tithe was given annually for the support of the local priesthood: "A tithe of everything from the land, whether grain from the soil or fruit from the trees, belongs to the LORD; it is holy to the LORD. Whoever would redeem any of their tithe must add a fifth of the value to it. Every tithe of the herd and flock—every tenth animal that passes under the shepherd's rod—will be holy to the LORD" (NIV). This is similar to a church budget. The second kind of tithe, to underwrite the expenses of the three major Jewish festivals of Passover, Feast of Tabernacles, and Feast of Weeks, is found in Deuteronomy 12:5-19 and 14:22-27. Today, church funds are seldom spent for religious celebrations, except banquets and fellowship. The third tithe identified in Deuteronomy 14:28-29 and 26:12-15 was taken every third year for local communities to help the needy. Today, this need is addressed by government programs, public charities like United Way, and benevolent and mission giving in the church. Therefore, the annual average of the tithe in the Old Testament equaled twenty-three and one-third percent of income before any buildings or special offerings.

In the New Testament, tithing is mentioned four times—in Matthew 23:23; Luke 11:42; Luke 18:12; and Hebrews 7:4-9. Tithing was the expectation in Jesus' culture, so it was not necessary for him to teach it. Paul and John do not provide specific teachings about the tithe, but they strongly address the issues of attitude and motives for giving.

An excellent consideration of the practice of tithing can be found in Chapter 5 of Robert Schnase's book *Five Practices of Fruitful Living* (Abingdon Press, 2010). Most denominations have expressed positions that affirm tithing or that establish tithing as a giving goal. A tithing lesson and a sermon manuscript are provided on the Resource CD-ROM, but each church must make a decision about tithing as an emphasis. (See Adult Lesson 3 and the Optional Sermon in the Worship and Teaching folder on the CD-ROM.)

Having established the background and biblical foundations for this program, this Program Guide will now provide specific directions for accomplishing each of the five steps. The accompanying Resource CD-ROM provides supplemental materials needed for implementation.

PLANNING AND IMPLEMENTING
THE PROGRAM

The *Extravagant Generosity* program is made up of five steps. The steps, listed below, are described in more detail in the following pages. A list of the steps and the tasks that make up each step can be found in the Pastor and Program Director Checklist on page 31.

Step 1: Decide
Present the program to leadership and approve dates.

Step 2: Assemble
Form the leadership team.

Step 3: Prepare
Equip the leadership team.

Step 4: Execute
Complete the planning function.

Step 5: Implement
Four Sundays of worship, preaching, storytelling, and teaching.

STEP 1

DECIDE:
Present the program to leadership and approve dates

The *Extravagant Generosity: The Heart of Giving* program is a theologically sound, creative stewardship approach, simple in design, and built around functions that are easy to understand and implement. The objective of this program over time, is to change the culture in your church from fund raising to generosity as a core value of discipleship. The effective methods and procedures can be used year after year to ultimately cultivate an environment of generosity.

Every church makes a decision about how to address annual tithes and offerings for ministry, what to do, and when. In some churches, this is a staff decision, and in others, a lay leadership group decides. Regardless, once direction is determined, an orientation for decision makers should be held to discuss the basic design of the stewardship program and objectives.

The orientation for decision makers should accomplish two purposes:

- Review the *Extravagant Generosity: The Heart of Giving* program and objectives. (Refer to the Timeline and review the Program Guide.)
- Approve the program schedule, including the four Sunday dates for implementing the program.

> Early in the process, determine the number of households to be included in the program. This is an important number, as it is the basis for setting printed materials quantities. This database starts with member families and should include regular attendees.

The Pastor should lead in selecting the best dates for the program and present these dates as part of the orientation. When selecting dates, start at the end of the process and work back toward the beginning.

Start by blocking out dates for the four Sundays the program will be presented. (See Step 5 in Pastor and Program Director Checklist.) The four Sundays chosen should coincide with traditionally high attendance times in the church. Determine the date for Sunday 4, Commitment or Response Sunday, and work back to set the date for Sunday 1, the beginning Sunday. Avoid holiday weekends, time change weekends, and other times when community events would negatively affect church attendance. Clear the church calendar of any events that may compete for focus, and activities that may require high-energy involvement from large groups of people. Once the dates are reserved, nothing should be added to the church calendar during that period.

STEP 2

ASSEMBLE:
Form the Leadership Team

Step 2 shapes the *Extravagant Generosity* Leadership Team and focuses on preparing the Narrative Scope of Ministries, a brief description of ministries in narrative form.

The Pastor's Role

The Pastor plays an important leadership role in the entire program, from initial adoption of the program and enlisting the director through leadership in worship and message. The Pastor's role includes the following key tasks:

Extravagant Generosity Leadership Team
Pastor
Program Director
Communication Team Leader
Leadership Summit Team Leader
Worship and Teaching Team Leader
Spiritual Emphasis Team Leader

- Enlist the Program Director. Work with the Program Director to identify and enlist the remaining Function Team Leaders.
- Plan worship and sermons in keeping with the generosity theme. (See Worship and Teaching folder on the Resource CD-ROM for sample sermon outlines.)
- Lead in forming the Narrative Scope of Ministries. (See Step 2: Assemble folder on Resource CD-ROM for a model.)
- Provide input for identifying guest list for the Leadership Summit—a special gathering of primary church leaders and spouses—and approve the final list.
- Participate on the Worship and Teaching Team, which includes worship, preaching, storytelling, and teaching.
- Find details of these responsibilities on the Pastor and Program Director Checklist, p. 31. (See Worship and Teaching folder on the Resource CD-ROM for supplemental materials.)

The Program Director's Role

The Program Director, the first leader recruited, will coordinate all areas and serve as the spokesperson for the initiative. The Program Director has the following key tasks:

- Serve as spokesperson to the congregation for the program.
- Assist the Pastor in forming the Leadership Team, making strategy decisions, and developing the Narrative Scope of Ministries.
- Participate on Worship and Teaching Team, which includes worship, preaching, storytelling, and teaching.
- Lead in enlisting storytellers with Pastor input.
- Monitor and oversee the work of the program teams, through five "show and tell" meetings, which allow leaders to share progress.
- Specific details of these responsibilities are included on the Pastor and Program Director Checklist, p. 31.

There is one combined checklist for the Pastor and Program Director, as they work closely together as a team. Knowledge of respective roles and responsibilities strengthens mutual support. The responsibilities of the Pastor and Program Director may be refined or exchanged, depending on individual preference, skills, time, and interest.

Finding the Right Leaders: Qualities and Skills

The success of the *Extravagant Generosity* program depends to a large extent on finding and equipping the right leaders for the leadership team.

Program Director Qualities and Skills

The Program Director should have a strong commitment to generosity, be a faithful giver, and have a sincere desire to encourage generosity in the church. Important qualities include organizational skills, willingness to follow the clear plan outlined in the program, and effective communication skills.

Team Leader Qualities and Skills

Team Leaders should possess the gifts, skills, and graces to best lead the four defined functions. The team may consist of one lay or staff person and a small ad hoc team or an appropriate existing leadership group. Encourage leaders to expand their teams and involve more people, if desired. Following are ideal qualities and skills for Team Leaders:
- Communication Team Leader: Computer skills; administrative skills; ability to develop and follow the details of production schedule, including assembly and distribution of materials at designated times.
- Leadership Summit Team Leader: Gift of hospitality; ability to plan an

enjoyable event for church leaders, including the details of location, food, decoration, invitation, and attendance building.

- Worship and Teaching Team Leader: Management skills, ability to see the big picture and coordinate input from other teams as their work impacts the four Sundays of worship, preaching, teaching, and story-telling. This team leader also works closely with the Pastor and Program Director in identifying storytellers; discussing worship ideas; and encouraging and assisting in the use of lessons with leaders of adults, youth, and children.
- Spiritual Emphasis Team Leader: Excellent communication skills, spiritually mature, known for personal commitment and interest in prayer, and ability to encourage others to participate in the spiritual emphasis plan. This team leader also assists in creating displays.

Development of the Narrative Scope of Ministries

Identifying the correct leaders for each team is the first step in the program. The Pastor and the Program Director must next develop the Narrative Scope of Ministries. This is a strategically important communication tool to convey ministry accomplishments and hopes. Find further guidelines and a sample format on the Resource CD-ROM, along with helpful worksheets (see Step 2: Assemble folder on the CD-ROM). This is a key element in the *Extravagant Generosity* program. This is not a line-item budget, or a page of items with detailed financial information. It is the story of the church's ministry and a vision for the future.

We recommend that the Pastor speak with the leader of the Finance Committee and/or other areas of financial responsibility to explain the Narrative Scope of Ministries approach: how it will be used and why it is important. Assure leaders that the Narrative Scope of Ministries will not replace any reports or documents they typically create and use in their fiduciary roles. It is a narrative to communicate the scope of ministries to the congregation. It would be a strategic error to omit this discussion.

Depending on the time of year the church implements the *Extravagant Generosity* program, the church budget may already be developed. If so, the budget becomes a resource for developing the Narrative Scope of Ministries. If not, information from last year's budget will provide needed reference for preparing the Narrative Scope of Ministries. Those responsible for developing the operational budget of the church may do so following completion of the program.

Practicing Extravagant Generosity: Daily Readings on the Grace of Giving

The Pastor and the Program Director should lead the way in encouraging churchwide, unified study and prayer. Through such efforts, God is honored and spiritual bonds are strengthened. The *Extravagant Generosity* program supports and encourages personal spiritual growth with the use of a devotional guide developed specifically for this program, *Practicing Extravagant Generosity: Daily Readings on the Grace of Giving,* by Robert Schnase.

A congregation working together through this devotional book sharpens church-wide focus and contributes to consistency of the message. In subsequent years, as your church continues to use the *Extravagant Generosity* program, you may desire to use other related works by Robert Schnase, such as *Five Practices of Fruitful Congregations, Five Practices of Fruitful Living, Cultivating Fruitfulness: Five Weeks of Prayer and Practice for Congregations, Forty Days of Fruitful Living: Practicing a Life of Grace,* and *The Balancing Act: A Daily Rediscovery of Grace,* all published by Abingdon Press.

Technology in Communication

The Pastor and Program Director should encourage the use of all available communication technology within the church's ability. Technology has revolutionized the way people give and receive information, register for events, and conduct personal business. According to recent studies done by the Pew Internet & American Life Project, e-mail has become the preferred way to receive information, with well over 90 percent of adults ages 18-72, and 79 percent of adults 73+ using e-mail ("Generations Online in 2009," Pew Internet & American Life Project, by Sydney Jones and Susannah Fox, Jan. 28, 2009). On percent of adults ages 18 and older get religious information from the Internet ("America's Online Pursuits," Pew Internet &American Life Project, by Mary Madden and Lee Rainie, Dec. 22, 2003). A well-planned, brief biweekly e-mail from the Pastor builds relationships and connection, especially in larger congregations. These often contain points of celebration, an important aspect of church life, and highlights for the next Sunday sermon.

Social networking tools are another valuable communication venue in the church. The Pew Internet & American Life Project Surveys also indicate 67 percent of Gen Y (ages 18-32), 36 percent of Gen X (ages 33-44), and 20 percent of the Younger Boomers (ages 45-54) use social networking to stay connected ("Generations Online in 2009," Pew Internet & American Life Project, by Sydney Jones and Susannah Fox, Jan. 28, 2009). People in these age groups indicate the connection is more important than the information itself. There is a longing to connect. Texting is another tool that allows the church to create presence and send specific messages to targeted audiences. Whether used to share a prayer thought of the week during the *Extravagant Generosity* program or a brief encouraging message, such tools can be very beneficial for church branding and connection.

Technology has opened new and cost-effective ways to communicate, involve people, and encourage generosity. Tithes and offerings can be scheduled online, thus providing regularity of gifts from some members. Members can register for special events and more. Online giving, debits, and many other giving options are not merely for the convenience of members. They are enormously beneficial to the church, significant factors in leveling out the traditional summer slump in tithes and offerings. Do not expect significantly higher member participation through such tools the first year or two. Educate members, and eventually a significant portion of giving will come as a result of these tools.

When Step 2 tasks are completed, including the formation of the Leadership Team, Narrative Scope of Ministries, and information regarding the number of households in your church, the framework is in place to proceed to Step 3.

STEP 3

PREPARE:
Equip the Leadership Team

Once the *Extravagant Generosity* Leadership Team is in place, the Program Director, with Pastor input, arranges a time for orientation of the Leadership Team. The Pastor and Program Director plan the orientation using the agenda provided on the Resource CD-ROM (see Step 3: Prepare folder on CD-ROM). This initial gathering of the Leadership Team affords the Pastor and Program Director an opportunity to express appreciation and sets the tone for the program to be a positive, enriching experience for both the church and the Leadership Team.

In preparing for this important formation meeting, adopt the perspective that team members want to be successful in their roles. Consider four dynamic motivations for accepting the invitation to be a part of the Leadership Team:

1. The desire to be part of a positive approach to encourage generosity in the congregation
2. Personal involvement spans a defined, brief period of weeks
3. A program and a step-by-step plan are provided
4. There is a team, working together

The Pastor and Program Director contribute greatly to the Leadership Team's overall success in the following ways: support the team in prayer, communicate with the team as recommended, assist when needed, and encourage the team. Involvement for the Leadership Team is an act of personal generosity. William James said, "The best use of life is to spend it for something that outlasts it." Only the Kingdom of God outlasts — everything else vanishes. The mission of the church is to share the love, forgiveness, and grace of Jesus Christ. Encouraging generosity is Kingdom building.

- An agenda to guide the orientation is on the Resource CD-ROM.
- Use the PowerPoint presentation on the Resource CD-ROM to present an overview of the program and objectives.
- Provide Function Team leaders with copies of their respective sections in the Extravagant Generosity Program Guide. Focus on the Timeline and on the importance of using the checklists that are provided.
- Identify dates for "show and tell" meetings of the Function Team leaders.

STEP 4

EXECUTE:
Complete the Planning Function

Step 4 is a five-week preparation period. The Program Director convenes "show and tell" meetings with Team Leaders. These gatherings should be weekly during the five-week preparation period, as indicated on the Timeline. The maximum time limit for these meetings is ninety minutes. These are not working sessions, but times for sharing updates, monitoring progress, and indicating areas where assistance may be needed. These team gatherings support Team Leaders and build camaraderie. Team Leaders work independently with their teams during this period. (See the Resource CD-ROM for comprehensive ideas, timelines, and tools, formatted and ready for use by teams.)

The Timeline provides a sense of the rhythm of how the Teams work as they relate and coordinate with one another. Also see the overview of the work of each in this Program Guide, in the section Program Teams and Tasks.

As Step 4: Execute is nearing completion, two important things will occur in preparation for Step 5: Implement:

• Two weeks before Sunday 1, the first mailing goes out to homes. It will include the Pastor's letter, the devotional guide, and Heart Card #1 "What do you love most about our church?" Letters and Heart Cards are in the Communications folder on the Resource CD-ROM. The devotional guide should be on order.

• One week before Sunday 1, the church Leadership Summit is held. See details in the Leadership Summit section (p. 43). Find tools in the Leadership Summit folder of the Resource CD-ROM. The Spiritual Emphasis Team may also have special prayer activities planned leading into Sunday 1. (See the Spiritual Emphasis folder on the Resource CD-ROM).

STEP 5

IMPLEMENT:
Four Sundays of Worship, Preaching, Storytelling, and Teaching

Sunday
1

WORSHIP—EKG: MINISTRY FLOWS FROM THE HEART
- Preaching—Sermon Text—1 Timothy 6:17-19
- Take-Away—Sharing and good deeds result in caring ministries
- Visual—Bulletin insert and/or slides for screens about your church family's good deeds and caring ministries
- Celebrate—Things we love about our church
- "What's It All About?"—Program Director describes program, Leadership Team recognized
- Optional—Children and youth involved in worship and children's moment coordinated with worship theme

STORYTELLING— "WHERE HAVE YOU SEEN JESUS AT WORK TODAY?"

TEACHING—LESSONS IN SUNDAY CLASSES OR SMALL GROUPS
- Lessons for adults, youth, and children on the Resource CD-ROM
- NOTE: Additional, full lessons for use in small groups are available in the *Small-Group Leader Guide*
- Narrative Scope of Ministries available in gathering area

MONDAY AFTER SUNDAY 1:
- Mail letter #2 and Heart Card #2, "Who in our church family has made a difference in your spiritual life?" to return in worship on Sunday 2.

Sunday
2

WORSHIP—THE ART OF LOVE: RELATIONSHIPS ARE MATTERS OF THE HEART
- Preaching—Sermon Text—John 13:34-35
- Take-Away—Your relationships with one another prove you know God
- Visual—Bulletin insert and/or slides for screens that show God's love working through relationships and ministries
- Celebrate—People who have extended Christ's love to us
- Acting in Love—Commitments due from church leaders
- Optional—Children's moment coordinated with worship theme

STORYTELLING—"WHO HAS MADE A DIFFERENCE IN YOUR SPIRITUAL LIFE?"

TEACHING—LESSONS IN SUNDAY CLASSES OR SMALL GROUPS
- Lessons for adults, youth, and children
- NOTE: Additional, full lessons for use in small groups are available in the *Small-Group Leader Guide*

MONDAY AFTER SUNDAY 2
- Mail letter #3 with Narrative Scope of Ministries and Heart Card #3, "What is your vision and hope for our church?" to be returned in worship on Sunday 3

Sunday
3

WORSHIP—BUCKET LISTS: VISION AND HOPE ARE INSPIRATIONS OF THE HEART

- Preaching—Sermon Text—Joel 2:28; Matthew 6:33; Colossians 3:1
- Take-Away—God-sized vision requires faith and stepping out of your comfort zone
- Visual—Bulletin insert and/or slides for screens describing fruitful ministries made possible by great vision and hope
- Celebrate—Sources of hope in your life and visions for the future
- Recognize—Announcement of church leader participation
- Optional—Children's moment coordinated with worship theme

STORYTELLING—"WHAT IS YOUR VISION AND HOPE FOR OUR CHURCH?"

TEACHING—LESSONS IN SUNDAY CLASSES OR SMALL GROUPS

- Lessons for adults, youth, and children
- NOTE: Additional, full lessons for use in small groups are available in the *Small-Group Leader Guide*

MONDAY AFTER SUNDAY 3

- Mail church family letter #4 with Estimate of Giving Card and Narrative Scope of Ministries, in preparation for Sunday 4

Sunday
4

WORSHIP—DECLARATIONS OF YOUR HEART: EXTRAVAGANT GENEROSITY IS AN EXPRESSION OF YOUR HEART
- Preaching—Sermon Text—John 3:16; 2 Corinthians 8:24
- Take-Away—Well done, good and faithful servant
- Celebrate—God's provision is trustworthy, and our heart controls our treasure
- Visual—Bulletin insert and/or slides for screens expressing generosity

STORYTELLING—"WHAT INFLUENCED YOU TO STEP OUT OF YOUR COMFORT ZONE TO EXPRESS YOUR LOVE FOR GOD WITH GENEROUS GIVING? HOW IS IT WORKING FOR YOU?"

TEACHING—LESSONS IN SUNDAY CLASSES OR SMALL GROUPS
- Lessons for adults, youth, and children
- NOTE: Additional, full lessons for use in small groups are available in the *Small-Group Leader Guide*

EXPRESSING YOUR GENEROUS HEART—MOMENT OF COMMITMENT

Follow-up Stage: What Happens after Sunday 4?

A primary focus throughout the four weeks of the *Extravagant Generosity* program is to celebrate God's provision through personal spiritual enrichment and become a more generous people. Some tasks are needed to close out the program. Beyond that, the church should pursue intentional efforts to retain and nurture new thoughts about giving and generosity on a year-round basis. Some closure tasks include:
- Invitation to respond with Estimate of Giving Cards and envelopes placed in the offering plate in worship on following Sundays
- Follow-up mailing to those not responding as of eight days after Sunday 4
- Interim and final reporting in person from the pulpit, by the Pastor and Program Director, to celebrate and to encourage those who have not responded

- Interim and final reporting in all other communication venues, focusing on positive results (e.g., percentage of congregation responding, benchmarks achieved) cast in the context of Heart Card stories
- The final communication from the pulpit should take place approximately one month after Sunday 4
- Express appreciation by sending a letter of acknowledgment for gifts
- Continue using storytelling once a month to celebrate God's work in the lives of members
- In your evaluative process during Step 2, there may have been needs identified related to technology to support generosity and ministries of the church. Address these in the coming months so these tools can be in service as soon as possible

Concluding Observation About Sundays 1–4

Beyond implementing the *Extravagant Generosity* program, the key for cultural change is creating an environment and activities that lead individuals to embrace generosity as a tenet of their faith experience. The motivation for generosity lies in the heart; this is consistently confirmed by Scripture. Our hearts and treasures are inextricably linked. Through sermons, Bible study, storytelling, and communication, people will be encouraged to consider God's call on their hearts and have an opportunity to respond.

People experience the message in different ways. Each element in the *Extravagant Generosity* program has an intentional purpose. From the use of *Practicing Extravagant Generosity: Daily Readings on the Grace of Giving* to sharing what we love about our church and take-away truths from worship, all program elements work together to influence the heart and to create a spirit of gratitude.

Any program or plan can be made less effective by changing or altering elements and not adhering to key principles. When elements are omitted, the results will be sacrificed. Your diligent efforts to follow the plan and use the various features and suggestions will result in optimal response and will lay a strong foundation for the future.

Remember, the intent is not to focus on money or raise funds to support the budget, but to encourage heart change and embrace generosity as a core value of personal discipleship. Then, generosity will occur.

Pastor and Program Director Checklist

WHEN	WHAT	WHO	DEADLINE
Step 1 Decide	**Before orientation meeting**		
	Review Timeline, Program Guide, and Resource CD-ROM. Set dates for the 4 weeks for program implementation	Pastor	
	Identify and enlist PD	Pastor	
	Review Timeline, Program Guide, and Resource CD-ROM	PD	
	Orientation meeting		
	Program and dates formally approved	Pastor, PD	
	Hold orientation for church staff. Request 6–10 key points or ministry benchmarks to be used as needed in materials by Prep Week 3. Discuss use of social media tools (which, how, when, and who will be responsible for e-mail, tweets, Facebook updates, and blogs)	Pastor	
Step 2 Assemble	Identify and enlist Team Leaders for Communication, Leadership Summit, Worship /Teaching, and Spiritual Emphasis	Pastor, PD	
	Determine number of households in database	Pastor, PD	
	Evaluate and determine capacity to use church website, e-mail, texting, and other technologies for communication; follow through with appropriate people	Pastor, PD	
	Review and facilitate acquisition of *Practicing Extravagant Generosity: Daily Readings on the Grace of Giving*	Pastor, PD	
	Discuss Narrative Scope of Ministries with groups that need to know approach (such as finance team)	Pastor	
	Develop Narrative Scope of Ministries	Pastor, PD	
	Identify guest list for Leadership Summit for Function 2 Team Leader	Pastor, PD	
	Schedule and invite Function Team Leaders to orientation	Pastor, PD	
Step 3 Prepare	Hold orientation for Function Team Leaders	Pastor, PD	
	Set dates for "show and tell" Function Team meetings	PD	

WHEN	WHAT	WHO	DEADLINE
Step 4 Execute	**Prep Week 1**		
	Review Function 1 production schedule with Function 1 Team Leader, Pastor, and PD letters; confirm mailings	Pastor, PD	
	Challenge adult teachers to teach lessons provided	Pastor	
	Provide roster of Leadership Team to Function 1 Team to include on letterhead	Pastor, PD	
	Prep Week 2		
	Identify and enlist storytellers (through Prep Week 3)	Pastor, PD	
	Plan worship and sermon for Sundays 1–4 (through Prep Week 4)	Pastor	
	Obtain, review, and return master letters to Communication Team Leader	Pastor, PD	
	Review Leadership Summit and confer with Leadership Summit Team Leader	Pastor, PD	
	Confirm use of children and youth cards, lessons, worship participation, letter to parents; advise Communication Team Leader for production purposes	Pastor, PD	
	Prep Week 3		
	Work with Leadership Summit Team Leader to plan program	Pastor, PD	
	Prepare storytellers (through Prep Week 4)	PD	
	Plan details of card collection and display for Sundays 1–3, confer with Spiritual Emphasis Team Leader (through Prep Week 4)	PD	
	Prep Week 4		
	Confirm teacher plans to use lessons provided	PD	
	Brief Leadership Summit program participants, and meet with Leadership Summit Team Leader to confirm details	Pastor, PD	
	Determine report date and communicate results in newsletter, visuals, and in worship	Pastor, PD	

WHEN	WHAT	WHO	DEADLINE
	Prep Week 5		
	Determine details for Sunday 4, Commitment/ Response Sunday, review materials needed	Pastor, PD	
	Monday of prep week 5 (2 weeks before Sunday 1), first mailing to church members, Function 1 Team	PD	
	Sunday of Prep Week 5, encourage use of Practicing Extravagant Generosity: Daily Readings on the Grace of Giving in worship	Pastor	
	Sunday of Prep Week 5: Leadership Summit	Pastor, PD	
	Determine strategy to follow-up with absentees from Leadership Summit	Pastor, PD	
Step 5 Implement	Sunday 1 Introduce program, PD, and Leadership Team	Pastor	
	Monday after Sunday 1 Program Director sends e-mail or note to church leaders encouraging them to return Estimate of Giving Cards by Sunday 2 (see Function 1 folder, Optional Letters subfolder on CD-ROM)	PD	
	Sunday 2 Report results of church leader participation	Pastor	
	Sunday 3 Confirm logistics for Sunday 4, moment of commitment	Pastor, PD	
	Sunday 4 Expressing Your Generous Heart—Moment of Commitment	Pastor	
	Monday after Sunday 4 Confirm Pastor's appreciation letter to participants being sent and the Financial Secretary's letter	Pastor, PD	
	Sundays 5 & 6 Verbal invitation to respond two Sundays following Sunday 4	PD	
	Year-round Continue using storytelling as a part of worship	Pastor	

PROGRAM TEAMS AND TASKS

COMMUNICATION TEAM

*"The LORD's promises are pure,
like silver refined in a furnace,
purified seven times over." (Psalm 12:6 NLT)*

The Communication Team is responsible for producing all materials needed for the program. The materials are production-ready, except for the Narrative Scope of Ministries. For that document, the Pastor, Program Director, and staff will prepare and provide finished copy to the Communication Team. Worship folder inserts are completed on one side, leaving the back open to include specific ministry accomplishments in various ministry areas.

The quality of printed materials sends a message of importance. Attractive materials invite readership and need not be costly. The choices of paper stock, ink colors, and layout all set the tone for quality. Be committed to the task of producing materials that represent the church well. Stick closely to the models provided.

The Communication Team will likely be the largest team. The distinctive tasks fit well with a sub-team approach, with some team members designated for assembly and others for production and distribution. It would be wise to include a member of the church office staff on the team, because each day the church conducts administrative functions similar to those the Communication Team implements. For example, most churches have a group that assists in preparing church mailings. In essence, they are an assembly team. Tap into already existing groups to assist as needed. The production schedule allows advance scheduling to avoid last-minute crises.

Using Outside Vendors

Some materials can be produced in the church office, and other pieces may need to be sent to outside vendors for printing. At the outset, the Communication Team Leader should talk with the staff and determine the church's printing capability and available equipment. Professional printers are not necessarily cost-prohibitive. Often high-volume copy jobs are more cost-effective when taken out of house, if high-speed quality equipment is not available at the church. The cost of supplies and operating your printers or copier must be considered in evaluating and comparing true costs. Four important factors to consider when use of an outside vendor may be helpful:

- Other demands on the church's equipment, as regular church operations should not be displaced
- Availability of staff assistance to use the equipment, if necessary
- Specifications for printed items, such as Estimate of Giving Cards
- Deadlines for production, as delayed production of materials will have a negative result on momentum. Production benchmarks are set and must be met

Obtain two to three bids before selecting a vendor. To prepare for the bid request, print out copies of all materials for reference and use the materials quantities checklist. Provide the printer with a copy of the item from the Resource CD-ROM in the bid process. A vendor who refuses to create a quote based on sample materials and quantities does not want your business; move on to someone else.

Both the church and the vendor need a working relationship to be successful. The Communication Team Leader's goal should be to equip the vendor to succeed by communicating in writing, noting clear deadlines, and following up.

Some vendors, especially small shops, may accept more business than can be handled, and then become overloaded. The type of equipment in the small shop often presents limitations. Be straightforward in talking with professional printers during the bid stage about cost and delivery deadlines. Quantity and price are important. The least expensive bid is not always the best. Ask the vendor for cost-saving tips.

Ask the church staff for names of any outside printers the church has used and their assessment of the quality and timely delivery of the vendor. If there is someone in the church who has a printing business, request a bid. The exception may be if the individual anticipates providing the service as a gift-in-kind to the church. Avoid places that specialize in "quick copies" for mass production, as they "copy" instead of printing. Typically, printing is more cost- effective for quantities.

Tips for Working With Outside Printers

- **Never give the printer the only copy of a document.**
- **Do not allow the printer to change the layout of materials, as all designs are intentional.**
- **Files may be sent by e-mail to the printer, making the process easier and more efficient.**
- **Establish a clear understanding of who is responsible for final proofing. If there is an error in the final product, and the church signed off on the item, giving approval/release to the printer, the church pays for it.**
- **Provide specific deadlines and quantities in the bid request, which must be in written form to avoid confusion.**
- **Do not give your absolute deadline to the printer, and do not use it for in-house productions. Expect the unexpected. Equipment breaks, people get sick, and delays happen, so plan and work in advance.**

Design and Layout of Materials

All printed materials used in the campaign should be coordinated and appear as part of the same "family" of materials. For example, use the same color paper, card stock, envelopes, and ink colors. This helps achieve branding for generosity. In the future, when people see the logo, they automatically associate and connect with generosity concepts.

Pay attention to the specified dimensions for items, such as the Estimate of Giving Cards, Heart Cards, and envelopes. Various Program Teams will submit items for production and distribution. For example, the Leadership Summit Team will provide copy for an invitation with quantities needed and deadlines. The Spiritual Emphasis Team may provide items to assist with spiritual emphasis. Each will be aware of quantities and distribution methods. Inquire about these early.

Robert Schnase's book *Practicing Extravagant Generosity: Daily Readings on the Grace of Giving* is available for ordering, so no printing will be necessary, just distribution. The Resource CD-ROM contains all needed materials in multiple formats when applicable, such as PDF, Word, and Rich Text Format (RTF). Most of the items are production-ready, though some require the addition of the church name and address.

A complete set of logos, in various formats such as JPEG and PNG, is included in the Communication folder on the Resource CD-ROM.

Communication Materials

- **Worship Guide Inserts:** The creation of final worship guide inserts may be a collaborative effort, involving the Communication Team, the Worship and Teaching Team, and church staff. Templates are on the Resource CD-ROM. One side of the inserts is complete, leaving the other side available for communicating and promoting ministry accomplishments and hopes. Be prepared at the first meeting to request six to eight key points or ministry benchmarks from various areas of ministry. The Worship and Teaching Team Leader is the primary contact for this. Communicate a deadline for receiving it. Ideas include: highlights from various areas of ministry; positive quotes taken from Heart Cards of children, youth, and adults; and Scripture passages and prayers to encourage generosity. (See the Spiritual Emphasis folder on the Resource CD-ROM.)
- **Narrative Scope of Ministries:** The narrative budget will be finalized early and given to the Communication Team for production. See the Communication Checklist (pp. 39–42) for the distribution timing of the Narrative Scope of Ministries and all other items.
- **Letterhead:** A letterhead format is in the Communication folder on the Resource CD-ROM. The Leadership Team will be listed down the left margin of the letterhead, as indicated on the letterhead template. Obtain these names from the Program Director to complete the letterhead. Produce all program-related letters on this letterhead.
- **Slides:** Templates for PowerPoint slides to use in worship are in the Communications folder on the Resource CD-ROM.

Getting Started

- The Communication Checklist provides a guide for planning. Begin by printing out copies of all materials on the Resource CD-ROM. Review each item and specifications.
- Review the suggested production and distribution schedules for various items.
- Set dates for production and distribution.
- Follow up with anyone who must provide final approval or specific items for production as follows:
  - Letterhead: Contact Program Director for team names.
  - Letters: Submit to Program Director and Pastor for review. Find out who should approve letters for children and youth, which accompany their Estimate of Giving Cards.

- Narrative Scope of Ministries document: Obtain from Program Director and Pastor.
- Worship guide insert: Obtain approval from Program Director and staff.
- *Practicing Extravagant Generosity: Daily Readings on the Grace of Giving* resource: Coordinate with Spiritual Emphasis Team Leader and Program Director.
- Leadership Summit invitation: Coordinate with Leadership Summit Team Leader.
- Talk with staff to evaluate in-house printing and copying capability and availability.
- Obtain any necessary bids from outside sources and choose vendor.
- Begin production of printed materials.

Communication Checklist:
Planning Materials and Quantities

All tasks listed take place in program Step 4: Execute

NOTE: Prep Week 1— Expand team as necessary and provide names to the Program Director. E-mail all letters to Pastor and Program Director for final approval.

PRINTING OR RECEIVING DEADLINE	QUANTITY RECOMMENDATION BASED ON # HOUSEHOLDS	QUANTITY ORDERED	ITEM	SPECIFICATION COMMENTS
Friday, Prep Week 1	# on Guest List plus 6–10 extras		Leadership Summit Invitation	4x6 nice white card stock
Friday, Prep Week 2	# on Guest List plus 6–10 extras		Catalog envelope for invitation to fit 4x6 card invitation, check size as there are more than one	White, with logo, no metal clasp
Friday, Prep Week 2	1.25 X # Households		*Practicing Extravagant Generosity: Daily Readings on the Grace of Giving* devotional guide (Obtain from Abingdon Press)	Purchase from Abingdon Press
Friday, Prep Week 2	1.25 X # Households		Catalog-sized envelopes for mailing devotional guide	White with logo and church's return address
Friday, Prep Week 2	2 X # Households		Adult Estimate of Giving Card	Tri-fold card, nice 8.5x11 card stock, color
Friday, Prep Week 2	# Youth plus 12 extra		Youth Estimate of Giving Card	Single card printed both sides, color
Friday, Prep Week 2	# Children plus 12 extra		Children's Estimate of Giving Card	Single card printed both sides, color
Friday, Prep Week 3	4.5 X # Households		Letterhead	White nice stock, logo, color
Friday, Prep Week 3	4.5 X # Households		# 10 letterhead envelopes	Match letterhead, logo, color, church's return address

Communication Checklist:
Planning Materials and Quantities
- Page 2 -

PRINTING OR RECEIVING DEADLINE	QUANTITY RECOMMENDATION BASED ON # HOUSEHOLDS	QUANTITY ORDERED	ITEM	SPECIFICATION COMMENTS
Friday, Prep Week 3	1.5 x # Households		#9 return envelopes	Printed with church's return address
Friday, Prep Week 3	1.5 x # Households		Adult Heart Card #1 "What do you love most about our church?"	White card stock, one side printing, color, must fit in #10 letterhead envelope
Friday, Prep Week 3	1.5 x # Households		Adult Heart Card #2 "Who in our church family has made a difference in your spiritual life?"	White card stock, one side printing, color, must fit in #10 letterhead envelope
Friday, Prep Week 3	1.5 x # Households		Adult Heart Card #3 "What is your vision and hope for our church?"	White card stock, one side printing, color, must fit in #10 letterhead envelope
Friday, Prep Week 3	# Children Kindergarten-level and above x 4		4 Children's Heart Cards	White card stock, one side printing, color, must fit in #10 letterhead envelope
Friday, Prep Week 3	# Youth x 4		4 Youth Heart Cards	White card stock, one side printing, color, must fit in #10 letterhead envelope
Friday, Prep Week 3	Average worship attendance x 4		4 Worship guide inserts	Sized to fit nicely in worship guide, two-sided printing, color
Friday, Prep Week 3	50% of the # Households		Dedication card to use on Sunday 4 for members already responding	Pastel blue paper, one side printing, one color, print three-up on single page
Friday, Prep Week 3	1.5 x # Households		Narrative Scope of Ministries	Check with staff for final dimensions, white paper, color, folded

Communication Checklist:
Assembly, Content, and Distribution

REFERENCE ITEM	WHO RECEIVES	DISTRIBUTION METHOD AND CONTENT	YOUR ASSEMBLY DEADLINE DATE	TARGET PROGRAM DISTRIBUTION DATE	ACTUAL DISTRIBU- TION DATE
Leadership Summit Invitation	Church leaders	• Mail • Invitation only	Assembly Date	Monday, Prep Week 3	9-16-13
EG-Y, Estimate of Giving Card, youth	All youth	• Mail or hand out in youth group • Letter provided	Assembly Date	Monday after Sunday 3, Hand out distribution option: Sunday 3	
EG-C, Estimate of Giving Card, children	All children, kindergarten & up	• Mail or hand out in Sunday school or Children's church • Letter provided	Assembly Date	Monday after Sunday 3, Hand out distribution option: Sunday 3	
CL-1 Letter, Estimate of Giving Card	Adults attending Leadership Summit	• Given out • CL-1 Letter, Narrative Scope of Ministries, return envelope • (Give to the Team Leader for the Leadership Summit)	Assembly Date	Leadership Summit; Sunday Prep, Week 5	
CF-1 Letter, Church family, first mailing	All households	• Mail • CF-1 Letter, Devotional guide, Heart Card #1 "What do you love most about our church?"	Assembly Date	Monday, Prep Week 5	
Sunday, Prep Week 5	Leadership Summit				
CF-2 Letter, Church family, second mailing	All households	• Mail • Letter, Heart Card #2 "Who in our church family has made a difference in your spiritual life?"	Assembly Date	Monday after Sunday 1	

Communication Checklist:
Assembly, Content, and Distribution
- Page 2 -

REFERENCE ITEM	WHO RECEIVES	DISTRIBUTION METHOD AND CONTENT	YOUR ASSEMBLY DEADLINE DATE	TARGET PROGRAM DISTRIBUTION DATE	ACTUAL DISTRIBUTION DATE
CF-3 Letter, Church family, third mailing	All household	• Mail • Letter, Narrative Scope of Ministries, Heart Card #3 "What is your vision and hope for our church?"	Assembly Date	Monday after Sunday 2	
CF-4 Letter, Church family, fourth mailing	All homes, except those attending the Summit, as they already have this	• Mail • CF-4 Letter, Adult Estimate of Giving Card, return envelope	Assembly Date	Monday after Sunday 3	
Follow-up letter 1	Non-respondents	• Mail • Letter, Estimate of Giving Card, and return envelope	Assembly Date	8 days after Sunday 4	
PA-1, Pastor's letter of appreciation	Members responding	• Mail • Letter only • Confirm Letter Sent	Assembly Date	Week after Sunday 4 and continue as cards are received	
PA-2, Pastor's letter of appreciation	Entire Program Leadership Team	• Mail or e-mail • Letter only • Confirm letter sent	Assembly Date	Day after team orientation	
Children's Heart Cards	Children, kindergarten & up	• Hand out in Sunday school classes, children's church	Assembly Date	Provide to Spiritual Emphasis Team Leader for distribution	
Youth Heart Cards	Youth	• Hand out in Sunday school classes, youth group	Assembly Date	Provide to Spiritual Emphasis Team Leader for distribution	

LEADERSHIP SUMMIT TEAM

"If your gift is to encourage others, be encouraging. If it is giving, give generously. If God has given you lead ership ability, take the responsibility seriously."
(Romans 12:8, NLT)

Modeling the Practice of Generosity

It has been said that a leader knows the way, shows the way, and goes the way. Leader actions are louder than mere words. The primary responsibility for influencing generosity in the congregation lies with those already entrusted with leadership roles. It is essential that the Pastor, staff, and church leadership teams become advocates and change agents to influence and create a positive environment for nurturing generosity. If you are serious about becoming a more generous congregation, with resources to advance ministry and higher levels of involvement, appoint leaders who model this attribute.

Affecting change of any type is gradual, and requires intentional patience and commitment. There are no quick fixes in bringing about change. Embracing biblical truths about generosity and giving, forming new thoughts, and expressing new giving behaviors happens one person and one family at a time. When generosity takes root, you will know it. You will sense it in the spirit of the people. You will see it in joyful conversations and expressions about the future. You will hear it in bold prayers and expressions of thanksgiving. It will be experienced in greater levels of involvement and giving. Intentional effort to talk about these important leadership issues is essential. The Leadership Summit is designed to allow these conversations to happen.

This may be the first time your church leaders have been challenged to be the first to participate. It may seem awkward to some. Others may discourage this leadership principle, to avoid being asked themselves. There may be some among current leadership who have not matured in their spiritual journey as faithful stewards, and others who do not give at all. *Extravagant Generosity: The Heart of Giving* is the starting point to cultivate generosity and the grace of giving in an intentional manner. Think of a pebble tossed into a lake. It forms concentric circles, radiating out from the center, until eventually it covers a great area on the lake's surface. The Leadership Summit is like that pebble. It creates a similar effect. When leaders develop a mindset of generosity and model giving, it spreads; soon the entire congregation is influenced by it. The Resource CD-ROM contains formats for the invitation, program, attendance-building e-mails, and a script for callers (see Leadership Summit folder), as well as Leadership Summit Checklists (see Step 3 folder and pp. 47-50 in this book).

Why a Leadership Summit?

The Leadership Summit brings a high degree of credibility and integrity to the generosity message to be shared with the congregation. This dynamic, face-to-face gathering is not business as usual and leaders know it. It creates a setting for fellowship, information sharing, storytelling, vision casting, and challenge. It provides an unprecedented opportunity to express appreciation, further inspire leaders in their roles, and cultivate relationships. It focuses on the powerful message that leaders must model the generosity they hope to see in their congregation. Giving inspires and creates giving.

Who plans this event, and when is it?

The Leadership Summit Team plans the Leadership Summit. This event should be held at the end of Step 4: Execute, on the Sunday of Prep Week 5. (See the Pastor and Program Director Checklist, p. 31.) This timing means the Leadership Summit can be completed before beginning the four Sundays of the program itself, and that leaders will have two weeks following the Leadership Summit to experience the program and participate in other spiritually enriching opportunities before returning their Estimate of Giving Cards on Sunday 2 of the program. On Sunday 3, the leaders' responses will be announced.

Where should the Leadership Summit be held, and what works best?

The Leadership Summit Team will determine the type of event, based on the culture of the church, number expected to attend, and location. The Leadership Summit may be held at the church or in a home. Both have advantages. Influencing factors are the number expected to attend, the type of event (dinner or reception format), and program needs. The home setting provides family-like surroundings. Service items can be available from the church, such as chairs and tables. If held in a home, the host should not be expected to cover the expense. This event is a legitimate expense and should be covered by the church. Either church or a home is preferred over a location that appears exclusive and expensive, unless of course a generous person provides the location as a gift. When blessed with such a gift, indicate this provision across the bottom of the invitation, "Location is provided as a generous gift from" (seek permission to use a name or simply say "a church family"). This will help diffuse criticisms that the church is spending too much money. Finding an appealing location is an added attraction for participation.

Who is invited to attend the Leadership Summit?

Invite church leaders, whether elected or appointed; those already involved with existing church leadership teams, such as governing boards, councils, finance, trustees, staff, are invited to attend with spouses. It is essential to include spouses, as decisions about generosity and stewardship affect the family and household. Spouses may become further inspired by the information shared and the vision cast. Additionally, a few other individuals who have historically been strong supporters of the church may be invited, though careful consideration should be given to this. There should be a rationale to guide formulation of the list of those to be invited. Otherwise, how will you explain when someone asks, "Why wasn't I included?" Be careful to avoid creating the appearance of an arbitrary, exclusive environment.

Regarding individuals who have historically supported the church with their gifts, but who are not involved in leader roles, it is always advisable for the Pastor and/or member of the *Extravagant Generosity* Leadership Team to make personal visits. This is the best setting in which to express appreciation, discuss the future of the church, talk about generosity, deliver information, and challenge continued faithfulness in giving, separate and apart from the Leadership Summit.

How are people invited to the Leadership Summit?

An invitation will be mailed to homes, two to three weeks in advance of the event. To achieve the best possible participation, the Leadership Summit Team will implement a protocol for building attendance:

- Send an early "save the date—more to come" e-mail or card.
- Send the invitation.
- Use e-mail to promote and build attendance after the invitation has been sent.

- One week after the invitation is mailed, send an e-mail summary of the "who, what, when, and where" of the Leadership Summit. Ask leaders to e-mail back confirmation of attendance. Depending on available technology, an imbedded link makes it easy for people to "click" and respond or simply hit "reply."
- Make telephone calls to those who do not use e-mail.
- Send specific e-mail requests to group or committee leaders, to follow up with their respective groups, to emphasize the importance of the event, and to set a standard for 100 percent participation in the Leadership Summit.

See the Leadership Summit folder on the Resource CD-ROM for attendance-building tools, a sample invitation, and a program agenda for participants with talking points to prepare.

While it may seem like a good idea to promote the Leadership Summit at the congregational level, it can be confusing, as not everyone is invited. It is, however, a positive point to share general knowledge of this gathering of church leaders.

What about nametags?

Influencing factors to help make this decision are church size, number of worship services, and culture. The fact that spouses will be present adds yet another consideration. It is sometimes difficult to put a name with a face, and some guests may not know one another by sight. Nametags allow people to greet one another without the fear of calling someone by an incorrect name. A greeter can fill out the nametags as guests arrive, or make them out in advance and arrange them alphabetically on the sign-in table. Use bold markers to assure names can be easily read at a distance.

Who is responsible for the Leadership Summit program?

A well-planned agenda, with suggested timeframes for each component, is provided in the Leadership Summit folder on the Resource CD-ROM. The Pastor and Program Director share the responsibility for Leadership Summit program implementation. If you choose a dinner setting for this event, the Summit program can be printed without time allocations and placed on tables. In a reception setting, only program participants need a copy of the program with the time allocations.

What about absentee leaders?

The Pastor and Program Director should review the list of absentee church leaders and make a determination about how to deliver packets. Some packets will be mailed, others may be delivered personally, and some church leaders may drop by the church office for their packets. Regardless, the objective should be to get the packets into the possession of church leaders as soon as possible.

Planning for Next Year

The Leadership Summit is a strategy to use annually. It builds camaraderie, empowers leaders, and encourages generosity. It should always be a special event rather than merged into a meeting. Next year the venue may be different, but the basic program components should remain the same.

The Leadership Summit Team Leader may expand the team, adding people with similar skills and interests in keeping with the work of the Team. Avoid duplication by submitting names of friends you would like to invite to be on the team to the Program Director.

Leadership Summit:
Program Planning Outline

See the Leadership Summit folder on the Resource CD-ROM for program agenda with talking points.

Welcome & Opening Remarks	(To be determined)
Invocation	(To be determined)
Celebrating Faithfulness, Opportunities, and Provision (media)	(To be determined)
Vision for Ministries in the Coming Year (Present and review the Narrative Scope of Ministries)	(To be determined)
(My Story—insert title for personal journey to grow in generosity)	Program Director
Personal Remarks and Set Tone for Challenging Leaders (insert title)	Pastor
Why Us, Why Now? (Leadership Challenge)	Program Director and Pastor
Practicing Extravagant Generosity: Daily Readings on the Grace of Giving	Spiritual Emphasis Team Leader and Program Director
Frame a Prayer for the Next Four Weeks	Spiritual Emphasis Team Leader and Program Directors

Leadership Summit Checklist: Scheduling

PROGRAM DATE	ACTUAL DATE	TASK
Prep Week 1		Expand team as desired and provide names to Program Director
Prep Week 1	*next EG meeting* *8/6 or 8/8*	Deadline: Confirm list of church leaders to invite to Leadership Summit, see Program Director, and send Leadership Summit invitation for production to Communication Team Leader Review tools on Resource CD-ROM and identify any which need approval of the Pastor and Program Director (agenda, invitation) and confer with Communication Team Leader
Prep Week 1		Event location determined; room reserved (if applicable)
Monday, Prep Week 2	*Mid-Aug.*	Deadline: 1st e-mail blast or card—"Save the date"—to guest list Arrange for childcare: nursery, older children, with appropriate snacks and activities ✗
Prep Week 2		Caterer bids obtained for comparison, if using outside source, review and select provider, or determine food and preparation
Thursday, Prep Week 2		Deadline: Invitations printed and ready to address
Friday, Prep Week 2		Address invitations
Monday, Prep Week 3	*9-16-13*	Deadline: Mail Leadership Summit invitation
Friday, Prep Week 4	*~~9-27~~ 9-23*	Deadline: 2nd e-mail blast or card—"Did you get your invitation? If you have already responded 'yes,' thanks. If not, let us hear from you" (Send the week after invitations are mailed)

Leadership Summit Checklist: Scheduling

- page 2 -

DEADLINE DATE	TASK	PERSON ASSISTING
Prep Weeks 3–4	Fun activities for children planned and assigned *Amanda ?*	
Prep Weeks 3–4	Follow up to see if media presentation will be prepared and used for event, make plans accordingly for room set-up, screen, someone to operate media presentation	
Prep Weeks 4–5	Table chart for room set-up prepared and given to appropriate people for configuration of tables to accommodate program	
Prep Weeks 4–5	Nametags, registration with sign-in sheet, permanent markers, trash can for nametag backs, and greeters arranged	
Prep Weeks 4–5	Extra table for packet display	
Prep Weeks 3–4–5	Plans set and assigned for using e-mail and other attendance-building activities to promote participation	
Prep Weeks 3–4–5	Plans confirmed and assigned for addressing invitations to accommodate Monday, Prep Week 3 mailing date	
Prep Weeks 4–5	Table/room decorations planned and assigned to create festive atmosphere of hospitality	
Prep Weeks 4–5	Program finalized and ready to produce, per type of program (reception or dinner)	
Prep Weeks 3–4–5	PA system, and confirmed person who will operate system, scheduled	
Prep Weeks 3–4–5	Confirm plans with greeters to lay out packets for distribution	
Prep Week 5	Parking already available or arranged, with attention given to those with limited mobility	
Prep Week 5	List of persons requiring transportation prepared after calls, and given to person who needs it to schedule	
Prep Week 5	Discuss packet layout with those assisting	
Prep Week 5	E-mail reminders and confirmation of details to those assisting	

Leadership Summit Checklist: Distributing Packets

METHOD OPTIONS FOR DISTRIBUTION	PROS	CONS
OPTION 1 : Hand out packets at the point in the program when the leader challenge is given	People not required to drop by a table on the way out the door People have packets to look at when speaker is giving challenge Packets can be arranged in seating order to expedite distribution	More assistance is needed to hand packets out quickly so the program does not lag Assistance needed to pull and arrange packets by seating order to expedite delivery
OPTION 2 *(Recommended):* Display packets alphabetically on tables, with name labels in clear view	Packets are not displayed when program begins to avoid early pick-up Greater control, more orderly, packets not lost or laid aside and forgotten People can find their own packets with minimum assistance, if any Guests pick up packet when leaving	Tables needed for display Few people needed to assist in laying out packets Someone at the table to assist, if needed
OPTION 3: Give packet to people at registration	No further contact People have packets to look at when speaker is giving challenge	Packets get set aside, lost, contents separated, and sometimes left behind Guest must manage packet while visiting and eating; some may leave early having received it People not listening to speaker, looking at packet

Displaying Packets Checklist: Do's, Don'ts, & Tips

- Do have adequate table space for laying out packets to avoid overlapping as this slows down pick-up.
- Do display packets after the program begins, to avoid early pick-up.
- Do have a few greeters at the table to assist, if needed.
- Do have a few generic packets available should someone show up you were not expecting, or have remaining member packets available to pull from.
- Depending on the number of leaders attending the church Leadership Summit, do consider arranging display tables so people can walk around all sides. If your group is large, separate tables rather than arranging them end to end to facilitate traffic flow.

- Do not stack or leave packets in a box and expect guests to sort through them. This creates a bottleneck and frustrates those waiting in line.
- Do not lay out the packets ahead of time or play favorites by giving some packets to friends as they arrive; others will wander by and expect the same.
- It is not necessary to sign a sheet to pick up a packet. You already have the registration form and the packets are personalized.

WORSHIP AND TEACHING TEAM

"Take the things you heard me say in front
of many other witnesses and pass them on to
faithful people who are also capable of
teaching others." (2 Timothy 2:2)

The Worship and Teaching Team focuses on planning the four Sundays during which the *Extravagant Generosity: The Heart of Giving* program is implemented. Worship, preaching, storytelling, and teaching coalesce to create an inspirational, meaningful, and fruitful experience for members and visitors. Whether in worship, a small group, or Bible study, the message will be communicated in various ways to people of all ages.

The Worship and Teaching Team Leader interfaces with leaders of the other teams; their tasks are important to successful implementation of Worship and Teaching. For example, Communication sends Pastor and Program Director letters, Leadership Summit plans the Summit, and Spiritual Emphasis may have input for worship. The Worship and Teaching Team Leader becomes a point of contact and support for Sunday school teachers, storytellers, and those involved in worship planning.

Weekly e-mails, blogs, tweets, and Facebook updates can build expectancy and nurture thoughts on generosity. The Team Leader coordinates these with appropriate staff, the Pastor, and Program Director.

The Program Director and Pastor are closely involved with this team. Neither, however, should be the team leader. Specific responsibilities are identified on the Worship and Teaching checklist. Begin by reviewing the checklist to gain a sense of how coordination of various tasks with key leaders assures the best possible experience.

Among the numerous resources for the Worship and Teaching Team are sermon outlines; worship resources; Sunday school lessons for adults, children, and youth; guidelines for storytelling; ideas for collecting and using stories on-line; and more. The checklist that follows describes use of these resources, which can be found on the Resource CD-ROM.

NOTE: Also see the *Small-Group Leader Guide* that offers adult sessions with themes linked to the weekly worship themes, and the devotional readings in *Practicing Extravagant Generosity: Daily Readings on the Grace of Giving.*

Worship and Teaching Checklist

PROGRAM	ACTUAL DATE	TASK	RESPONSIBILITY & RESOURCE
Prep Week 1		Expand team as required and provide names to Program Director (PD)	Team Leader
Prep Week 1		Meet with the Communication Team Leader to review materials that need signatures or input to finalize and produce	Team Leader, PD
Prep Week 1		Follow up with Pastor and Program Director for approval of letters, and return letters to Communication Team Leader	Team Leader
Prep Week 1		Assist Communication Team Leader in proofing materials for production	Team Leader
Prep Week 1		Request by e-mail 6–10 key points of ministry accomplishments from staff and/or ministry leaders (missions, adults, children, youth) for use in side two completion of worship guide inserts Sundays 1–4. Obtain by Prep Week 3	Team Leader follow up with Pastor, PD
Prep Week 1		Determine which social media tools can be used; how, when, and who will be responsible for e-mail, tweets, Facebook updates, and blogs	Team Leader follow up with Pastor, PD
Prep Week 1		Discuss how Sunday school teachers will be contacted and prepare and provide copies of lessons for adults, children, and youth to leaders; follow through with communication plan	Team Leader, PD
Prep Week 1		Talk with Spiritual Emphasis Team Leader about Heart Card displays and provide team assistance in preparing space and creating displays for visuals	Team Leader, PD

Worship and Teaching Checklist
- Page 2 -

PROGRAM	ACTUAL DATE	TASK	RESPONSIBILITY & RESOURCE
Prep Weeks 1– Sunday 4		Pray for teachers of adult lessons on Sundays 1–4	Program Director (PD), Worship and Teaching Team, Spiritual Emphasis Team
Prep Week 2		Confirm plans to involve children in worship on Sundays 1 and 4. Determine how youth can be involved Confirm use of Estimate of Giving Cards, and letter will be prepared for children and youth Advise Communication Team Leader of quantities for production Obtain and review letter to parents of children from Communication Team Leader, discuss with Program Director and Pastor, send letter	Team Leader, Pastor, PD confer with leaders of children and youth
Prep Week 2		Enlist storytellers and create a roster of Sunday assignments	PD
Prep Week 2		If possible to videotape storytellers, schedule time. Talk with storytellers and provide tools to guide preparation. Set date to meet with storytellers in Prep Week 4 (group setting preferred, as they may glean pointers and encouragement from one another). Provide names of storytellers to Communication Team Leader to be included on worship guide inserts	Team, videographer
Prep Weeks 2-3		Follow up with Spiritual Emphasis Team Leader about spiritual emphasis plans related to worship, advise the Pastor and Program Director about plans, schedule plans	Team Leader, PD, Spiritual Emphasis Team Leader
Prep Week 2		Plan worship period for Sunday 4, the Moment of Response when members return Estimate of Giving Cards, logistics, and what will make it most meaningful, special liturgies, or remembrances, etc.	PD, Pastor
Prep Week 3		Determine whether PowerPoint slides will be used in lieu of printed inserts	Team, PD, Pastor
Prep Week 3		Finalize plans for Sunday 4, response period, determine what assistance will be needed for response on Sunday 4	PD, Pastor, Team

PROGRAM	ACTUAL DATE	TASK	RESPONSIBILITY & RESOURCE
Prep Week 3		Coordinate obtaining and using stories in the newsletter and on the website, and the creation of a storybook on website	PD, Team
Prep Week 4		Assist with first mailing of materials	Communication Team, Worship & Teaching Team
Monday, Prep Week 4		Meet with storytellers, if they are not videotaped, for final briefing	PD
Monday, Prep Week 5		Possible date for first e-mail/blog/tweet/Facebook update with prayer thought (watch for your Heart Cards and devotional guide)	Team Leader follow up with person assigned
Monday, Prep Week 5		Leadership Summit	
Monday before Sunday 1		Possible date for e-mail/blog/tweet/Facebook update with prayer thought	Team Leader follow up with person assigned
Monday before Sunday 2		Possible date for e-mail/blog/tweet/Facebook update with prayer thought Program Director sends e-mail or note to church leaders encouraging them to return Estimate of Giving Cards by Sunday 2	Team Leader follow up with person assigned
Monday before Sunday 3		Possible date for e-mail/blog/tweet/Facebook update with prayer thought	Team Leader follow up with person assigned
Monday before Sunday 4		Possible date for e-mail/blog/tweet/Facebook update with prayer thought	Team Leader follow up with person assigned
Sundays 1–3		Available on Sundays to assist in worship, and as greeters at Heart Card locations and displays throughout the week	Team assists Spiritual Emphasis Team
Thursday before Sunday 4		Obtain Estimate of Giving Cards, return envelopes, and dedication cards in worship area (chair/pew racks, etc.) for Sunday 4	Team
Week before Sunday 3		Schedule follow-up in worship, announcements of progress, celebrations for the next four weeks	PD, Team
Monday after Sunday 4		Replenish supply of Estimate of Giving Cards and return envelopes in worship area	Team

After making decisions about plans and materials needed to support the work of your team, submit requests for needed funding by e-mail to the Program Director, and confirm at "show and tell" meeting of Function Team Leaders.

SPIRITUAL EMPHASIS TEAM

"Your prayers and your compassionate acts
are like a memorial offering to God."
(Acts 10:4)

Prayer is essential in the believer's relationship with God. Prayer opens our hearts and minds to spiritual discernment and generosity. The Spiritual Emphasis Team will lead the church in activities that encourage prayer and study. The two primary elements around which all other spiritual emphasis features will be built are:

- *Practicing Extravagant Generosity: Daily Readings on the Grace of Giving*
- Heart Cards returned by members the first three Sundays of the program

Practicing Extravagant Generosity: Daily Readings on the Grace of Giving

Robert Schnase, author of *Five Practices of Fruitful Congregations, Five Practices of Fruitful Living,* and other works, has prepared an enriching personal devotional guide, *Practicing Extravagant Generosity: Daily Readings on the Grace of Giving.* This will be mailed or delivered to all member homes two weeks before the *Extravagant Generosity* program begins in worship. The Communication Team will distribute the devotional, and the Pastor and Program Director will encourage its use each week in worship.

Heart Cards

During the first three weeks of the *Extravagant Generosity* program, Heart Cards will be a focal point of celebration. Heart Cards encourage expressions of gratitude and strengthen connection. Celebrations in worship will include member expressions from the Heart Cards that have been returned.

- Sunday 1, Heart Card #1—What do you love most about our church?
- Sunday 2, Heart Card #2—Who in our church family has made a difference in your spiritual life?
- Sunday 3, Heart Card #3—What is your vision and hope for our church?

Heart Cards are also available for children and youth. These will be given out in classes and group meetings. Adults will receive their Heart Cards along with a letter. They are asked to drop off their cards each Sunday at a designated location where an appointed person will receive the cards. A Spiritual Emphasis Team member should be at all locations to greet members. Do not simply create a drop box; ask members to take cards to the church office, or have members drop the cards in the offering plate. Take this opportunity to extend hospitality.

Obtain extra cards to place in the worship area and at the locations where members will drop off cards on Sundays. Each week prior to worship, gather three or four cards for the Program Director to give to the Pastor for mention in worship. Get the cards back so they can be included in displays.

Displaying Heart Cards

The Spiritual Emphasis Team is responsible for gathering and displaying the cards throughout the church for members to enjoy. The Worship and Teaching Team Leader is available to assist with displays.

A walk-through of the church buildings will be helpful in identifying the best, high-traffic locations for creating displays of cards. If the church display boards are cluttered, clear off the boards to make space for the Heart Card displays, for greater focus. Discuss any needs for clearing space with the Program Director and determine a plan to accomplish the task. Removing items may be a sensitive issue for some, so it is important to observe correct protocol before temporally removing them.

Discuss preference for displaying children and youth cards with leaders, as they may desire to display Heart Cards in their respective areas. If that is the case, request a few to include in the primary displays in the high-traffic areas of the buildings. The Heart Cards are in the Communication folder on the Resource CD-ROM.

Each Sunday, gather the cards and add to the displays. It is usually best to design displays with a variety of cards rather than one subject. Other uses for Heart Cards include:

- Transfer comments to a PowerPoint slide to be used on screens each week.
- Submit some of the Heart Card comments to be included in the church newsletter.
- Create a "Heart" storybook on the website and post cards there.

Talk with the person in charge of the church's webpage to create a link called "Heart Stories," using the *Extravagant Generosity* logo as an icon to assist with branding. By clicking on the link, members may share: special prayer thoughts and Bible passages, member Heart Card stories, and member quotes

Once the *Extravagant Generosity* program concludes, Heart Cards can remain on display for a few weeks. At the designated time, the Spiritual Emphasis Team should remove all displays and provide the cards to the appointed person in the church office for future use. The "Heart Stories" may remain on the website year-round.

The Spiritual Emphasis Team may also desire to do other types of activities to involve people of all ages. There are key times in the four-week program that are well suited for some of these ideas. For example, the eve of kickoff is a perfect time for a prayer event. Another time for a prayer event is the week leading up to Sunday 4.

Review the numerous optional ideas for all age groups in the Spiritual Emphasis folder on the Resource CD-ROM and determine which to implement in your church. As you review the following ideas, present those that involve worship to the Pastor:

- Prayer Chain Links or Bookmarks
- Churchwide Moments of Prayer
- Existing Groups
- Newsletter and Website
- Social Networking and Media
- A Place for Prayer
- Drama
- Visible Reminders of Prayer
- Prayer Chain
- Prayer Walk
- Prayer Tree
- Prayer Crosses in Bloom
- Prayer Stones or Prayer Hearts
- Prayer Booklet
- Organize a Prayer Event (also includes ideas for children and youth)
- Prayer Poems
- Prayers for Children and Youth
- Create a Prayer for the *Extravagant Generosity* program

Spiritual Emphasis Checklist

All tasks listed take place in program Step 4: Execute and Step 5: Implement
NOTE: Prep Weeks take place in program Step 4: Execute. Sundays 1–4 take place in program Step 5: Implement

Program Date	Actual Date	Task	Responsibility & Resource
Prep Week 1		Expand team as necessary and provide names to Program Director	Team Leader
Prep Week 1		Designate visible, high traffic location(s) where members will return Heart Cards; communicate this to the Program Director, as this location is included in the letters to be mailed to members	Team Leader with Worship and Teaching Team Leader
Prep Week 1		Identify locations for displays throughout the church in traffic areas so cards can be seen, determine types of displays (wallboards, movable displays, easels, decorated screens, etc.)	Team Leader with Worship and Teaching Team Leader
Prep Week 1		Review *Practicing Extravagant Generosity: Daily Readings on the Grace of Giving* devotional guide in order to promote use	Team Leader
Prep Week 1		Review and choose spiritual emphasis ideas to implement with all ages, discuss plans with Pastor and Program Director, put all spiritual emphasis dates on the church calendar	Team Leader
Prep Week 2		Enlist a slate of greeters to be at the Heart Card drop-off location(s) to receive cards on Sundays 1–3	Team Leader confer with Worship and Teaching Team Leader
Prep Week 2		Begin organizing prayer events planned for the Saturday before Sunday 1 of the program Contact youth leaders to discuss ideas for involving youth in their own prayer event, set date, and communicate youth involvement in the church newsletter	Team Leader
Prep Week 2		Contact leaders of children about their involvement in art projects (such as creating leaves for a prayer tree); discuss ideas about their prayer event, set date, and communicate children's involvement in the church newsletter	Team Leader

Spiritual Emphasis Checklist
- Page 2 -

Program Date	Actual Date	Task	Responsibility & Resource
Prep Week 3		Confirm Worship and Teaching Team assistance in card collection on Sundays 1–3 and creation of displays	Team Leader
Prep Week 3		Publicize prayer events and advocate participation	Team Leader
Prep Week 4		Obtain Heart Cards from Communication Team Leader to provide to leaders of children and youth, confirm distribution and collection plan for displays	Spiritual Emphasis Team Leader with Worship and Teaching Team Leader
Prep Week 5 leading up to Sunday 1		Obtain Heart Card #1 "What do you love most about our church?" from those attending the Leadership Summit, in order to create early displays the week leading up to Sunday 1	Team Leader confer with Function 2 & 3 Team Leaders
Monday, Prep Week 5		Distribution of church family letter #1 with *Practicing Extravagant Generosity: Daily Readings on the Grace of Giving*	Team Leader confirm with Communication Team Leader
Sunday, Prep Week 5		Leadership Summit	Team Leader confer with PD about agenda
Sundays 1–4		Pray for Pastor, worship, storytellers, and teachers	Team with Worship and Teaching Team
Sunday 1		Team at drop-off location for Heart Cards Place extra blank Heart Cards in the worship area, classrooms, and in the locations where cards will be dropped off. Prior to worship, give the Pastor 3 or 4 cards that may be mentioned in worship	Spiritual Emphasis Team Leader confer with PD and Worship and Teaching Team Leader
Sunday 2		Team at drop-off location for Heart Cards Place extra blank Heart Cards in the worship area, classrooms, and in the locations where cards will be dropped off. Prior to worship, give the Pastor 3 or 4 cards that may be mentioned in worship	Spiritual Emphasis Team Leader confer with PD and Worship and Teaching Team Leader
Sunday 3		Team at drop-off location for Heart Cards Place extra blank Heart Cards in the worship area, classrooms, and in the locations where cards will be dropped off. Prior to worship, give the Pastor 3 or 4 cards that may be mentioned in worship	Spiritual Emphasis Team Leader confer with PD and Worship and Teaching Team Leader
Sunday 4		Assist in worship as needed	Spiritual Emphasis Team Leader confer with Worship and Teaching Team Leader

After making decisions about plans and materials needed to support the work of your team, submit requests for needed funding by e-mail to the Program Director, and confirm at "show and tell" meeting of Function Team Leaders.

Resource CD-ROM Contents

Some resources on the CD-ROM are provided in multiple formats to allow usage on various types of equipment.

FOLDER	ITEM
Step 1	• Timeline

Step 2	• Checklist for Pastor and Program Director
	• Narrative Scope of Ministries
	   • Creating Narrative Scope of Ministries
	   • Narrative Scope of Ministries Format
	   • Scope of Ministries Worksheet
	   • Worksheet for Allocations with Notes

Step 3	• Leadership Team Orientation
	   • Leadership Team Orientation Agenda
	   • Leadership Team Orientation Slides
	• Communication Team
	   • Communication Team Forms
	   • Communication Team Guide
	• Leadership Summit Team
	   • Leadership Summit Team Forma
	    • Leadership Summit Team Guide
	• Worship and Teaching Team
	   • Worship and Teaching Team Forms
	   • Worship and Teaching Team Guide
	• Spiritual Emphasis Team
	   • Spiritual Emphasis Team Forms
	   • Spiritual Emphasis Team Guide

Communication	• Overview and Checklists
	• Logo Formats
	   • Adobe Illustrator
	   • JPG
	   • PNG
	• Worship Guide Inserts
	   • Creating Worship Guide Inserts and Use of Digital
	   • Worship Inserts (4)
	• Digital Signage for Screens
	• Estimate of Giving Cards
	   • Adult Card
	   • Adult Card Online
	   • Cildren's Card
	   • Children's Letter
	   • Youth Card
	   • Youth Letter
	• Dedication Card for Sunday 4
	• Church Leadership Letter (CL–1): Goes with the Estimate of Giving Card and Narrative Scope of Ministries to church leaders at Leadership Summit
	• Church Family Letters
	   • Church Family Letter 1 (CF–1): Mailed with *Practicing Extravagant Generosity: Daily Readings on the Grace of Giving* devotional guide and Heart Card #1 "What do you love about our church?"
	   • Church Family Letter 2 (CF–2): Mailed with Heart Card #2 "Who in our church family has made a difference in your spiritual life?"
	   • Church Family Letter 3 (CF–3): Mailed with Narrative Scope of Ministries and Heart Card #3 "What is your vision and hope for our church?"
	   • Church Family Letter 4 (CF–4): Mailed to every home (except church leaders who have already turned in Estimate of Giving Card) with Estimate of Giving Card and return envelope

FOLDER	ITEM

Communication	• Follow-up Letters
	  • Follow-up 1: Letter to non-responders who do not regularly give
	  • Follow-up 1A: Letter to faithful givers who typically do not return an Estimate of Giving Card
	• Optional Letters
	  • Financial Secretary Letter
	  • Pastor Appreciation Letter (PA–1)
	  • Pastor Appreciation Letter to Leadership (PA–2)
	  • Reminder Letter from Program Director
	• Heart Cards – Adult
	  • Sunday 1: Love
	  • Sunday 2: People
	  • Sunday 3: Vision Hope
	• Heart Cards – Children
	  • Heart Card Collection and Display
	  • Letter or E-mail to Parents
	  • Sunday 1: Love
	  • Sunday 2: FROG
	  • Sunday 3: Be Generous
	  • Sunday 4: Best Gift
	• Heart Cards – Youth
	  • Sunday 1: Love
	  • Sunday 2: Makes Difference
	  • Sunday 3: Vision Hope
	• Letterhead and Envelopes

Leadership Summit	• Overview and Checklists
	• Attendance-building Materials
	  • Call Sheet Form
	  • Calling Script
	  • E-mail Blasts
	  • Leadership Summit Invitation
	• Instructions for Packet Distribution
	• Program Agenda for Leadership Summit

Resource CD-ROM Contents — *continued on next page*

Worship and Teaching	• Overview and Checklist
	• Storytelling
	   • Online Story Follow-up
	   • Story Web Form
	   • Storyteller Outline
	   • Storytelling Overview for Program Director
	• Sermon Outlines
	   • Sunday 1 – EKG: Ministry Flows from the Heart
	   • Sunday 2 – The Art of Love: Relationships Are Matters of the Heart
	   • Sunday 3 – Bucket Lists: Vision and Hope Are Inspirations of the Heart
	   • Sunday 4 – Declarations of Your Heart: Extravagant Generosity Is an Expression of Your Heart
	   • Tithing Is a Matter of the Heart (Optional Sermon)
	• Worship Resources
	   • Worship Litanies
	   • Digital Screens for Use in Worship
	• Adult Lessons and Questions
	(See also *Extravagant Generosity Small-Group Leader Guide*, which offers adult sessions with themes linked to weekly worship themes and devotional readings in *Practicing Extravagant Generosity* devotional guide)
	   • Lesson 1 – Extravagant Generosity: The Heart of Giving
	   • Lesson 2 – Mission Flows from the Heart
	   • Lesson 3 – Tithing Is a Commitment of the Heart
	   • Lesson 4 – Practicing Extravagant Generosity
	   • Discussion Questions
	• Children's Lessons – Grades 1-2
	   • Lesson 1 – God Is Generous to Us, and We Are Grateful
	   • Lesson 2 – A Generous Heart
	• Children's Lessons – Grades 3-4
	   • Lesson 1 – Jesus Talks About Treasures
	   • Lesson 2 – It's About Time
	• Children's Lessons – Grades 5-6
	   • Lesson 1 – God Is Generous to Us, and We Are Grateful
	   • Lesson 2 – A Generous Heart
	• Youth Lessons
	   • Lesson 1 – How Do You Think People Define You?
	   • Lesson 2 – Just Do It! Putting Words into Action
	   • Lesson 3 – Wise and Faithful

Spiritual Emphasis	• Overview and Checklist
	• Suggestions for All Age Groups (Optional)
	   • Prayer Poems
	   • Prayers for Children and Youth
	   • Prayers for Prayer Booklet or Walk
	   • Prayer Chain Links or Bookmark
	   • Other Ideas

Appendix	• Letters (all letters in one document) • Program Director GPS